For Nienke and Loeka
Let's take a vacation!

Copyright © 2018 Johan Idema

Concept and text: Johan Idema
(www.johanidema.net)
Translation: Tessera Translations
Layout: Thomas de Bruin, Studio Lomox

BIS Publishers
Building Het Sieraad
Postjesweg 1
1057 DT Amsterdam
Netherlands
T +31 (0)20 515 02 30
bis@bispublishers.com
www.bispublishers.com

ISBN 978 90 6369 493 7

Johan Idema

HOW TO BE A BETTER TOURIST

Tips for a Truly Rewarding Vacation

B/S

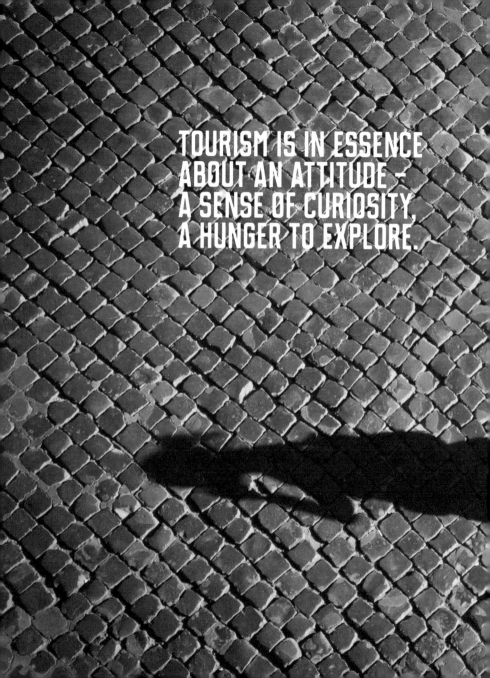

TOURISM IS IN ESSENCE
ABOUT AN ATTITUDE –
A SENSE OF CURIOSITY,
A HUNGER TO EXPLORE.

WHAT WAS ONCE A PRIVILEGE
TO BE FOUGHT FOR SEEMS NOW
TO HAVE BECOME A COMMODIT

THE TOURISM INDUSTRY
STILL BELIEVES FIRMLY
IN THROW-AWAY KITSCH
SOUVENIRS.

/zizii5tm
OURIS
THE
CIT

WHAT IF BEING A TOURIST IS SUDDENLY NO LONGER QUITE AS INNOCENT AS IT FIRST SEEMED?

VACATIONING IS ESSENTIALLY A HUMAN TRAIT, OFTEN ABOUT BREAKING WITH ROUTINES AND BEHAVIOR PATTERNS.

CONTENTS

CONTENTS

A FRESH LOOK AT VACATIONING

The problem of leisure
What to do for pleasure
– Gang of Four

Vacations are made of freedom. Pure freedom. Our busy lives, full of obligations, mean that a vacation is the only time we can do whatever we want, wherever we want. So how weird is it then that most of us spend that precious time doing the same things? That we descend *en masse* on the same cities, cluster around the same attractions and all visit the same picturesque neighborhoods, which can't actually handle the influx?

Is it because we all want the same things from our vacations? Perhaps. Is it because we never stop to think about how it could be done differently? Again, perhaps. But it certainly can be done differently and that's what this book is encouraging you to do. After all, what if all your trips seem to be getting more and more the same? What if being a tourist is suddenly no longer quite as innocent as it first seemed? Or what if your long list of must-sees is in fact stressing you out? As the writer Elbert Hubbard poignantly put it, "No man needs a vacation so much as the man who has just had one." *How to be a Better Tourist* takes a fresh look at making your vacation truly worthwhile and rewarding.

A brief history of vacation

Throughout history, humans have traveled the world. The idea of doing it for pleasure only really arose in the seventeenth century, though. That was when wealthy young men in Europe discovered traveling as a form of luxury and personal development. Until deep in the nineteenth century, it was normal for them to go on a *grand tour* of France and Italy, back to the artistic and cultural roots of western civilization. It was only much later, in the mid-twentieth century, that vacationing also became attainable for the working classes of the western world. Traveling let them compensate for the shortcomings of their everyday existence and they learned to live the lifestyle of a consumer society. This continued for about half a century, until it all began to snowball at the beginning of the twenty-first century. Plane ticket prices collapsed to unheard-of levels, journeys went ever further afield and more and bigger groups of tourists with a *Wanderlust* – including the new Asian middle classes in particular – came to the fore. Mass tourism was born.

Opening the hatches in your head
The one thing that has remained virtually unchanged all that time is why we take vacations. Traveling is essentially a search for new impressions, inspiration and meaning. Or, according to Professor Marli Huijer, "We've been telling each other for thousands of years about heroes venturing out into the world, discovering fantastic things and returning with wonderful tales. Only Odysseus or Aeneas used to be able to do that, but nowadays we can all travel and relive those heroic journeys. We too need to go beyond the horizons: that's where the adventures are that open up the hatches in your head. We think that'll make you a better person."

The high we can get from vacationing makes it a special and precious resource. The ancient Greek philosopher Aristotle called leisure time "our ultimate obligation", allowing us to reflect freely on our lives. Given the time and money we spend on traveling, though, it's safe to say that vacations are our ultimate form of leisure time.

Tourism as masturbation
The question is whether we take our ultimate obligation seriously enough. Our holiday travels are going further, but also focusing more on comfort and entertainment. We are traveling more often, but (as a result?) our vacations are becoming more similar. What was once a privilege to be fought for seems now to have become a commodity: a carton of milk we take from the shelf and then don't think about anymore.

We do make higher demands, though, expecting more from our trips. That creates a lot of stress. Even when planning the trip or hitting those final deadlines and packing the bags, and on the spot as well because of the queues, the crowded patios, or the bad weather. Then when you get back home, there'll be the stress of dealing with your e-mail backlog. Is it so strange that most heart attacks and burnouts now happen during our trips or in the three weeks afterwards? It's why Professor Ad Vingerhoets reckons that the usefulness of vacations is now hugely overestimated. "Lots of people can't cope with vacations at all. They impose lots of sights and activities on themselves, creating stress. I call that 'tourism as masturbation'. The fatigued body can't cope with the combination of mandatory relaxation plus the stimuli of a new destination."

A sector with a peculiar twist
All the journeys we permit ourselves to take add up to crazy amounts, worldwide. Like rising water levels and major migrant flows, a tsunami of tourists is also flooding our planet. Both the scale of mass tourism and its superficial nature seem to be becoming a global issue. Unrest bubbles beneath the

surface in many places. Residents are protesting against their cities being turned into fun parks, with signs saying 'Tourists go home'. Some European cities are attempting to control the human influx. Nobody is against tourism as such: everyone knows that it's a sector that helps increase prosperity significantly. But we'd like it to be more sustainable, because there's also no doubt that tourism has a peculiar twist. "Tourism is riddled with negative external effects," says the economist Frank Kalfshoven. "Both during the journey and during the stay, tourists like us are causing harm to people who are not involved in our vacations in any way. They don't benefit from them, but they are affected by them."

Add a little poetry to your trip

In short, anyone who opens their eyes to see how we approach our holiday travels will keep seeing things that astonish and worry them. It seems as if our vacations are in a loop without a pause button. If that's an issue you want to address in your own case, well, you're reading the right book. *How to be a Better Tourist* encourages you to think your vacations through more carefully, to explore alternative choices and so get more out of your trips. The assumption is that vacationing is essentially a human trait, often about breaking with routines and behavior patterns – the habits that you'll take along with you if you don't watch out.

Find out why you should perhaps stay at home. Understand why you also need to work while on vacation. Read why tourists should visit supermarkets and residential districts too. Our typical vacation behavior – visiting the maximum number of sights in the minimum time – is rarely the most rewarding. *How to be a Better Tourist* shows some possible alternatives. "The trick is no longer to go as far or as often as possible," notes one travel organizer, "but to add a little poetry to your trip." This book focuses on the essence of vacations: discovery, inspiration, variety, awareness and development. The tips that it presents are easy to put into practice and they aim to make a difference. Many of them are practical and focus on behavior; others sketch out an alternative way of thinking or mindset that can be just as beneficial while vacationing.

Is better also greener?

How to be a Better Tourist helps you get the most out of your trip without damaging the soul of your destination. Does that mean that better tourists are also greener? It doesn't directly tackle the issue of reducing the ecological footprint of your vacation, however, because it's pretty clear that staying at home impacts the environment least. *How to be a Better Tourist* is more about the sustainability of the content of your vacation – how you can genuinely make your trip a valuable, inspirational, and memorable experience. The choices needed for that often work out as greener and are in any event less damaging for your destination. This book will undoubtedly make you wonder whether all those holiday flights are really needed.

HOW TO READ THIS BOOK

Making your trip truly worthwhile is not about doing one thing right. Instead, it's about doing many things differently. So *How to be a Better Tourist* has not been written as a single, linear text for you to read from beginning to end. Instead, the book contains 28 suggestions – or strategies, if you like – that will help make your vacation more meaningful.

Each suggestion is meant to inspire or challenge you to evaluate your behavior to date, and explore your options for acting differently. Some of these tips tackle the choices you make at your destination; others focus on planning your trip or what to do when you get home again. You are welcome to read them in any order you like.

HOW TO BE

A BETTER TOURIST

TIPS FOR A TRULY REWARDING VACATION

THE PERFECT HOLISTAY

So you want to be a better tourist? Then there's no more logical place to start practicing than home. A vacation seems synonymous with far-away destinations, but tourism is in essence about an attitude – a sense of curiosity, a hunger to explore. Which you can do anywhere. So getting better at vacationing starts with a break at home. Or, as some English speakers might put it, a staycation or a holistay (though used here without any negative overtone of going cheapskate). →

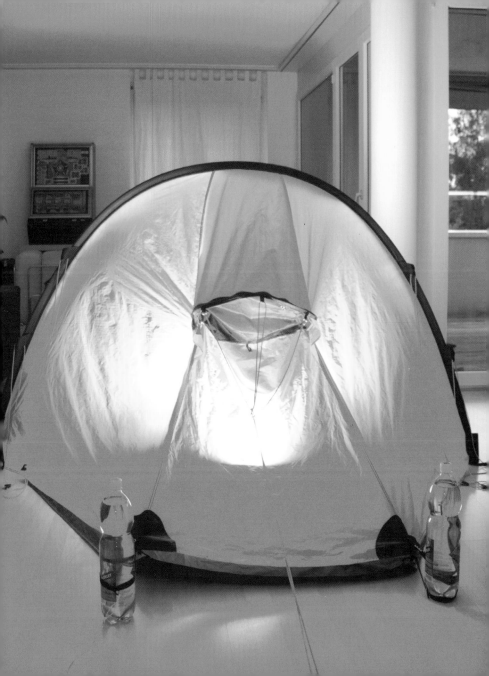

No stressing out at airports, gridlocked roads or noisy hotel guests – a holistay lets you avoid the downsides of mass tourism. And the stress. Because, as the tourism expert Greg Richards puts it, "The more commonplace vacationing becomes, the greater the stress." Without the urgency of taking in the must-see tourist items, the home vacation forces you to rethink thoroughly what a holiday actually means to you.

For some people, leisure time is about not having to do things. "As soon as I get the feeling that something is a must, I stop whatever it is," said a travel writer. "It's a feeling I refuse to accept. It takes away my freedom." The secret of a successful home break is above all to avoid your everyday routines. That requires discipline: keep your staycation different and fresh. The best way to do that is different for everyone, but don't be afraid to be as creative as possible. Get someone in to do the cleaning if you don't want to spend time on the washing. Get a friend round to cook for you. Go camp in your own garden. Or (a tip from an interior designer) turn your bedroom into a hotel room, including new bedlinen and flower petals.

A STAYCATION FORCES YOU TO RETHINK THOROUGHLY WHAT A HOLIDAY ACTUALLY MEANS TO YOU.

THE HOME-BASED TOURIST LEARNS ABOUT THE IMPORTANCE OF VARIATION AND THE CREATIVITY IMPOSED BY THE RESTRICTION.

Does a staycation mean staying at home indoors? Far from it, playing the local tourist gives you the opportunity to finally visit some of the treasures in your own area, which you may have been driving past for years. You'll be doing it deliberately too, just like the way things often impress us on our travels merely because we've taken time for a closer look. "The real voyage of discovery consists not in seeing new sights, but in looking with new eyes," as the philosopher Proust put it.

If you still think that holistays are boring or for losers, just try it. One staycation can do no harm, in between all those exotic holidays. Far-flung destinations are educational as well of course. But the home-based tourist learns better than anyone about the importance of variation and the creativity imposed by the restriction. Once you've got the hang of that, it becomes a valuable lesson that you can include in the baggage you take on vacation.

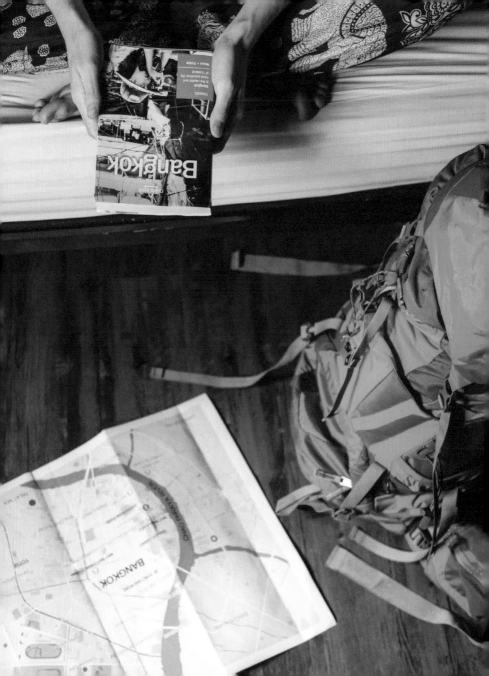

PRE-VACATION HAPPINESS

*"Well," said Pooh, "what I like best..."
and then he had to stop and think.
Because although Eating Honey was
a very good thing to do, there was a
moment just before you began to eat it
which was better than when you were,
but he didn't know what it was called.*
– A.A. Milne, writer

If you want to be a better tourist, be aware that looking forward to the fun makes it all the better. Studies have shown that we're often happier in the eight weeks before we leave than during the vacation itself. Interviews with 1500 people revealed that just planning or anticipating your trip can make you happier than actually taking it. Anticipation is half the fun.

So it's possible to enjoy a great vacation before you've even got there. How does that work? We build up positive expectations when we're looking forward to something, with our bodies making the same 'happy hormones' as during the actual event. That's true in other situations too. A piece of chocolate cake that you intentionally save for tomorrow is even more enjoyable.

Children are the champion anticipators. They let their fantasy run riot, getting the most out of the hoped-for experience. We adults need to relearn that trick. Practice makes perfect: once you've got the hang of it, pre-vacation anticipation hardly ever misfires. After all, unlike the actual vacation, you've got the fun parts totally under control.

Plan your vacation a long way ahead, so that you can enjoy it for longer. Talk plenty about your forthcoming trip, with colleagues, friends, and family. And of course, read about your destination, watch a movie that's set there, and try the local foods. Set up an obvious spot in your house a week or so before you leave to put the things you'll be taking. Every time you go past it, the promising sight of your holiday books or the smell of suntan lotion will crank your expectations up a notch.

The scientist Mark Mieras compares anticipation to a treasure you can always cherish and draw energy from. "It encourages you to cross boundaries, get moving and take a new step." Looking forward is perhaps one of the core essentials of human existence. If you can master the trick, your vacation will be more enjoyable. And your life will be too.

SICK ON ARRIVAL

Just a couple of days until your richly deserved vacation can begin. You make the final deadlines, pack your bags, get on the plane and... get sick the moment you're there. Dismayed, you spend the first few days in bed. The only thing worse than being ill is being ill on vacation. →

NO MATTER HOW PARADOXICAL IT MAY SEEM, RELAXING ON VACATION IS STRESSFUL FOR SOME PEOPLE.

Leisure sickness (starting your break being ill) was recently nominated by Webster's New World Dictionary as the new word of the year. But it's nothing new. Dutch research from 2001 has shown that 3% of Dutch people start their vacation with headaches, fatigue, muscle pains, and flu-like symptoms. So who on Earth falls ill when the fun can start? No matter how paradoxical it may seem, relaxing on vacation is stressful for some people. Your usual daily rhythm has gone; you're traveling to foreign climes, going out with the family or doing other things that you wouldn't always think were fun, at least at first. You're also eating differently, sleeping for longer and exercising more. Particularly for the first day or so, a sudden change in lifestyle can strain both mind and body.

But there's more to leisure sickness. "The simple idea we have – that when you are busy, your body is activated, and when you are not busy and have nothing to do, your body is relaxed – is simply not the whole story," according to Ad Vingerhoets, the professor who coined the term 'leisure sickness'. It's all about stress hormones. If we're under pressure, out bodies pump out adrenalin, making us more alert and more efficient. Cortisol is also released, which weakens the immune system. On vacation, stress falls away and adrenalin levels drop, suddenly leaving an excess of cortisol and compromising your resistance. That's what makes you more susceptible right at the start of your break.

Leisure sickness or not, plenty of people find that the first few days off simply fly by because they haven't caught their breath yet. So a more gradual transition from business to pleasure is always worthwhile. We tend to rush off the moment the last workday ends, but do you have to? Have a fun weekend at home first and then go – you'll surely be more rested.

Many test subjects who got rid of their leisure sickness had adapted their attitudes, for instance by treating their break less as a stress dump and more as a well-deserved gift that has to be 'accepted' with due care. The right mindset turns out to be just as crucial to a successful vacation as good planning is. Even more crucially, business and pleasure aren't as independent as they appear. They're actually closely interlinked variables, as satisfying work makes for better vacations. So perhaps being a better tourist actually starts with being a happy worker.

THE RIGHT MINDSET TURNS OUT TO BE JUST AS CRUCIAL TO A SUCCESSFUL VACATION AS GOOD PLANNING IS.

RENT A GERMAN

They're incredibly efficient, have great *bratwurst* and make the best cars. Those admirable attributes of Germans gave Johannes Blank – a German himself, 'as it happens' – the idea for an amusing website, www.rentagerman.de. It lets people hire Germans for meals, an afternoon's shopping or other "personal and social purposes." It was a conceptual stunt, but there turned out to be a real demand. People wanted Germans for odd jobs, parties, and planning vacations.

It's not only true for Germany, of course: inviting a native round can be a wonderful way of preparing for a trip to any destination. Anticipation is half the fun. On top of that, the quality of your trip is directly affected by the preparations. If you want to be a better tourist, take this stage seriously.

Personal stories and insights from someone born and bred in your holiday destination are way better than a travel guide on paper. Live narrators are efficient – listening is quicker than reading – and you can involve the whole group who are traveling. So that's more than enough reason to have a native round as a warm-up. Ask them to cook an authentic national meal, bring photos from their childhood or find a selection of YouTube clips that are typical of their country. Take time together and make things easy for your native by buying things in and driving them home afterwards.

The key advantage of a live guide is that they are interactive. You can lead the conversation round to what interests and fascinates you, so a successful evening also means asking the right questions. Sure, you want to know what the best museums and hotels are, but a guide book tells you that. The native lets you dig a bit deeper. What are the big issues and latest developments in the country? What are the typical good and bad sides of the locals? A clear analysis or background sketch will make more things (and different things) stand out on your trip.

If you don't know any Cubans, Swiss, or Vietnamese, your friends or work colleagues will. Facebook has a long reach: you'll find the native you're looking for there or elsewhere online – why not put a personal ad on an odd jobs website? Especially if you make it sound attractive: offer a home-made apple pie, a ticket for a popular local ball game, or some other suitable reward. The right, enthusiastic native will soon contact you.

BAD STUFF IS GOING TO HAPPEN

Disappointment is the mismatch between expectations and reality. You had looked forward to a perfect vacation – sun, fun, good food – but reality had other plans for you. It rained, there were mosquitoes, and you fell ill. Disillusionment is inevitable. →

Everyone faces disappointment every day. We simply expect too much. And if there's one thing we have great expectations of, it's our travels. "There's great pressure on making our summer vacations a success," says Professor Vingerhoets. "Everyone reckons they deserve it, so it's got to be fun and the weather's got to be great." On top of that, high expectations exacerbate the annoyances, such as long queues, poor service, or – you can't leave those problems at home – issues between you and your partner

The bizarre paradox is that vacation stresses you out more than the routine of daily living. The best thing a tourist can do is learn how to deal with expectations and disappointments. Lesson 1: you often expect too much from a holiday, so you're bound to be disappointed. It's smarter to lower your expectations. That's easier said than done, obviously, if you've paid good money for your trip and been looking forward to it for months.

What we anticipate from a vacation is driven by tempting photos of the destination and stories about how special it is. That's in the interests of the travel industry, because higher anticipations mean the destination will be reviewed as more attractive. Be aware of this and always do a reality check. Go to flickr.com (or other websites with user-generated content) and see what impression the genuine photos and travelers' tales give. You'll be dissatisfied less easily if your expectations are realistic.

"Expectation is the mother of all frustration," says the actor Antonio Banderas. Some people will recommend keeping expectations as low as possible, so that they're easy to exceed. That soon makes you indifferent, though, and spoils the

THE BIZARRE PARADOX IS THAT VACATION STRESSES YOU OUT MORE THAN THE ROUTINE OF DAILY LIVING.

THE BEST THING A TOURIST CAN DO IS LEARN HOW TO DEAL WITH EXPECTATIONS AND DISAPPOINTMENTS.

anticipation. Getting excited about a trip several times a day, which 40% of holidaymakers do, is recommended. Anticipation does generate passion and involvement. The best advice is therefore to cherish appropriate expectations. Don't just look forward to the highlights (often brief) but also remember that highs and lows are part of every trip. Vacations, after all, are packed with practical challenges in unknown territory. A hiccup, an unexpected event – bad stuff is probably going to happen at some point. There's no real way of avoiding it, but the right expectations will ease the disappointment.

The very idea that your mood and motivation are going to be put to the test when on holiday can be part of the anticipation too. So be selective and creative in what you expect. Check with traveling companions which prospects are pleasant and useful and which aren't. Choosing your expectations with care lets you choose how happy your vacation will be.

THE PRINCES OF SERENDIP

Ideally, our vacations would unfurl as a single, huge, spontaneous adventure, in which we move on happily from one surprise to the next. →

NOW THE MOST ESSENTIAL ITEMS FOR A SUCCESSFUL TRIP ARE PLANNING SKILLS.

That is after all when our travels are the best antidote to our over-organized lives full of deadlines. In reality, though, vacations keep getting more complicated, demanding ever more advanced logistics and technology. The most essential items for a successful trip are no longer suntan lotion or travel guides – it's different now: you need planning skills. More than ever, proper organization is make or break. Or, as the time management guru Alan Lakein would put it, "Failing to plan is planning to fail."

But what does good planning mean? When traveling, we are mostly planning how to fit sights into the available travel schedule: first Notre Dame, then the Eiffel Tower, then the Palais de Tokyo. However, if you pause to think about what really makes a vacation, you rarely come up with specific tourist must-sees. Ultimately we look for more general qualities in our travels, such as adventure, inspiration, or relaxation. Those are the goals that really need planning.

Have you ever unexpectedly found a picturesque square or a hidden restaurant? The *The Three Princes of Serendip*, a Persian fairy tale, calls this 'serendipity': a discovery that you weren't looking for. Strangely enough, the story sees serendipity as a skill, saying that clever and well-prepared people are more capable of discovering things by chance. That's where the fable touches upon the essence of planning for the qualities you want from a trip. Aspects such as inspiration and discovery can't be forced: they demand mental preparation and alertness above all. If you want a vacation full of (say) discoveries, be aware that getting lost can often be valuable (with hindsight), and embrace any unusual and unplanned events.

"Everyone has a plan till they get punched in the mouth," said the boxer Mike Tyson. Planning suggests that everything can be organized in advance, but that's only partly true for vacations. Be prepared for how you'll react if things go differently than expected. You can plan for that too. What do you do if the queues are too long, the weather won't play ball or you're suddenly exhausted? Take a book, or have alternative sights nearby up your sleeve. And above all, develop a mindset that makes you resistant and flexible, because the gods of misfortune never take a vacation.

ADVENTURE, INSPIRATION, OR RELAXATION, THOSE ARE THE GOALS THAT REALLY NEED PLANNING.

FUTURE MEMORIES

Vacations are where you make tomorrow's memories. Of all our leisure activities, our trips are the key moments we look back on in later life. Souvenirs perish, but memories generally stay. The stories we come home with often last for decades.

Memories are mostly made subconsciously, but not randomly. We recall some vacations clearly, but forget others almost at once. The most striking thing is that we often remember our travels with hindsight as more fun than they really were. That's why the philosopher Pieter Hoexum refers to vacations as nostalgia machines: "No matter how awful they were, time casts a golden glow over our memory of every vacation. Irritations large and small disappear and that morsel of happiness keeps growing in our recollections."

The first things we look for on our travels are entertainment and relaxation. But if the memories of a break are its most powerful aspect, shouldn't we use that more effectively? Memories affect how long you feel your journey to be, claims Marc Wittmann, author of the book *Felt Time: The Psychology of How We Perceive Time*. For the so-called 'classic holiday effect' – a break that feels much longer than it was – he recommends that you focus your vacation schedule less on quantity and more on quality. Because time stretches as you experience more memorable events. A plea, in short, to deliberately concentrate on the extraordinary, the things that are truly different from home. Those street cafes and restaurants might be enjoyable, but are they really memorable?

So, important criteria for vacations that stick in the memory are that they are deliberately and carefully chosen and distinctive. If what happens on the trip doesn't grab you, you won't remember it either. If you find yourself making lots of plans when you're already on vacation, it makes time rush by because you're mentally living in the future. Plan things before leaving, so that you can remain in the here and now at your destination. Help the process by taking 'mental snapshots' of special places: go sit down, take in the odors and colors and other details, and enjoy the moment. Take at least ten minutes, making a sound recording along with your mental photo if you need to (use your smartphone). Being more aware of the experience lets you enhance the enjoyment you get from your stay. If you think this sounds like an exercise in mindfulness, you're right. The better your vacation experience in the here and now, the more you'll enjoy it afterwards too.

SMALL TALK, BIG IMPACT

Our world is so saturated with smartphones that spontaneous chat seems to be on the verge of extinction. In trams, parks, or cafes, many people prefer their screens to contact with others. This is changing our vacations too, making interaction with the locals rarer. →

"I'd rather spend the whole day chatting to a guard or newspaper vendor than looking at church ceilings," said one travel author. Seasoned travelers often regard meeting other people as they go as one of their goals. They know that good travel memories depend on who you meet and not how many cathedrals or museums you visit. Noteworthy encounters are what make your recollections of a place stick. So while you're vacationing, be aware that every chat can be valuable, no matter how humdrum or awkward the start. "People are happier when they talk to strangers, even when they predict they'll hate it," says Kio Stark in his book *When Strangers Meet*. Any contact might yield nice insights or add an

unexpected twist to your day. How else would you have found that hidden courtyard garden, or learned why all the automobiles in the city have even-numbered license plates?

Getting a conversation going needs the everyday art of small talk: make eye contact, have a reason (no matter how simple), use humor, and listen carefully. It's at least as important that you are alone; a group, no matter how small, often hinders one-to-one contact. That can be awkward if several of you are vacationing as a group, so make agreements with the rest of your group that you get some time to yourselves – often a smart idea anyway (see tip 10).

GOOD TRAVEL MEMORIES DEPEND ON WHO YOU MEET AND NOT HOW MANY CATHEDRALS OR MUSEUMS YOU VISIT.

BE AWARE THAT EVERY CHAT CAN BE VALUABLE, NO MATTER HOW HUMDRUM OR AWKWARD THE START.

People with customer-facing roles, like waiters or store staff, are easiest to approach and often like helping others. They are a good source of up-to-date insider tips. Ask them about their favorite restaurant, the best park for a picnic or the prettiest sunset view. Or give them *carte blanche* and simply ask for their best tips.

Really valuable conversations go deeper. Those are held at 'slow' places like museums and parks, with cab drivers (see tip 19), retirees or others who are alone and have plenty of time. Challenging or original questions help you progress from small talk to meaningful conversation: they show you're interested and ready to listen. Be aware that a good conversation can't be forced; there'll be moments when you're given short shrift. But don't let that stop you: you're talking to a stranger and there's no need to be overly polite. You can stop whenever you want.

TO AIRBNB OR NOT TO AIRBNB?

The global rise of Airbnb and similar websites has been a wake-up call for the hotel industry. The platform, which lets people rent out their home like a hotel owner, has built up a large following in a short time. On any given night, one million people are staying in Airbnb homes. →

IF YOU WANT TO BE A BETTER TOURIST, THE KEY QUESTION IS HOW TO DEAL WITH AIRBNB.

Hotels do their utmost, but they can't provide the level of authenticity that Airbnb does. Pick well and an Airbnb lets you stay in real homes belonging to real people in real neighborhoods. Especially for longer vacations, it's more entertaining and often cheaper. It may seem for a short while as if you really live there, living that other life that you once dreamed of. Go as off-beam as you want: the platform offers a treasure trove of unusual, weird, experimental, and non-traditional places to live. You can live in an Airstream, a treehouse or a lighthouse, in a taxi cab in the middle of Manhattan, in a white cube gallery between artworks – you name it.

Renting out your house is an attractive source of income for the hosts. "Airbnb puts money in the pockets of local residents," a spokesman for Airbnb tells us. Even so, "living like a local" (the Airbnb promise) won't charm everyone. Critical residents say that the platform is pushing house prices up, causing a nuisance, disrupting communities in other words, playing into the hands of gentrification. And it's true that gentrification is on the march in many cities where Airbnb is popular – Amsterdam, Barcelona, New York. Is there an 'Airbnb effect,' stripping cities bare like a plague of locusts? That still needs to be studied, but a lot of experts already think that the platform is by no means a primary driver of gentrification.

If you want to be a better tourist, the key question is how to deal with Airbnb. Go along with the hype or not? Are you profiteering if you do? There's no denying that social sector housing also ends up on Airbnb, that houses are rented out permanently, and that single hosts may have multiple flats on offer at the same time. Dubious cases such as these are however often easy to spot and avoid. Genuinely authentic or unusual places to stay via Airbnb are mostly offered by real, enthusiastic owners. Sure, they're aiming to earn a bit on the side, but they are making their home available – usually only to a limited extent during their own vacations – with pride and dedication. Their homes are also easily recognizable on Airbnb and there aren't really any negative sides to renting them.

So the best Airbnb stays turn out to be the most socially responsible ones as well. Focus on finding them and you won't have to feel you're a locust. If your stay was satisfactory, do what you'd do if you borrowed anything else: write a thankyou note, leave a small gift, or bake a cake for your host. You're paying for the stay anyway, of course. But the trust that your host is placing in you, expecting you to treat their things as if they were your own, is at the heart of Airbnb. That is precisely what makes it different from hotels or other purchases. So it's only reasonable to show you appreciate that trust.

THE TRUST THAT YOUR HOST IS PLACING IN YOU, IS AT THE HEART OF AIRBNB.

A DAY ALONE

In *Alone in the World* by the author Hector Malot, the eight-year-old foundling Rémi has nobody. The boy roams the world for years, faces numerous setbacks and regularly bursts into prolonged bouts of tears. This heart-rending, almost sadistic youth road novel, mandatory reading for years at many schools, could well be one of the reasons why traveling alone is so unpopular.

On holiday with others – your partner, family, or friends– certainly has benefits. It's cheaper, more sociable and often simpler. But have you ever stopped to think about the flip side? Some sights such as art museums or a picturesque local cafe are better experienced alone. A good chat with a local (see tip 8) will hardly even happen if you're in a group. Travelling together also means making compromises, often messy ones that nobody is really happy with.

Does that mean vacationing alone is better? Not necessarily; setting out on your own isn't something everyone's cut out for. But there's a nice half-way house solution that's rarely used: an alone day. We often find it awkward to do our own thing in the company of others – it looks weird or anti-social. An alone day solves this elegantly. It's a good label to hang a group agreement on saying that everyone should get a bit of time to themselves, in the belief that it will benefit everyone. Spending all your time together for days or weeks on end can also easily lead to minor irritations. You may not want to put it that way, but a day alone can be a welcome cooling off period as well – a *leave-me-alone* day.

How can you enjoy a day's vacation on your own? Plan it, so that you're prepared. Take a full day and decide in advance on your own program. That shouldn't be difficult. You'll probably pick whatever the others will balk at – a special monastery, a spectacular fun park, or an afternoon's hassle-free shopping. Or choose something that's less easy to do in company: an afternoon reading a good book in a park, for instance. A day alone is also the perfect moment to give yourself a treat with a massage, a pedicure, or a good movie. "I restore myself when I'm alone," said Marilyn Monroe.

Paradoxically enough, meeting up with the group again is often the high point of a day alone. Nothing is better than sharing your adventures over the evening meal, realizing you should do it more often... and hesitantly admitting that you did actually miss each other. Just a little bit.

BUSINESS MEETS PLEASURE

For many people, vacations are to work as sex is to housekeeping. Everything you like about the one – exciting, adventurous and preferably on a tropical island – is missing in the other. It's not quite that black and white, of course. Holidays and work can go well together, though hardly anyone believes you should actually want them to. →

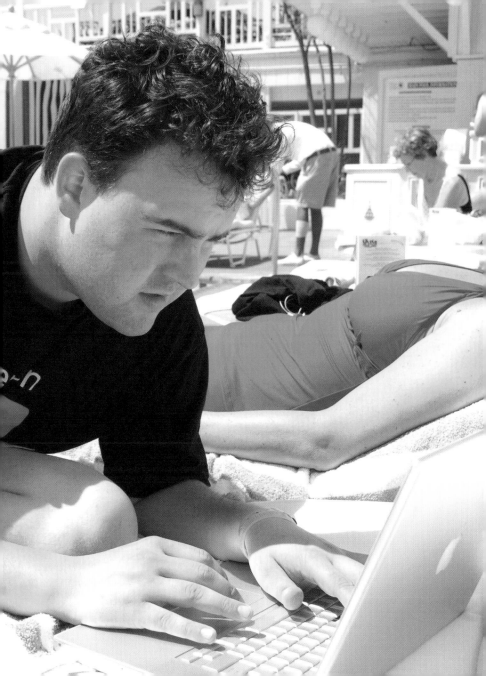

Studies have shown that more than half of us work while on vacation. Not for fun, but because the boss expects it or we don't want to feel guilty or look less dedicated. Or simply because vanity makes you think your colleagues can't cope without you. Working in your leisure time can be rewarding, though. Research suggests that preparation and discipline are needed: agree it with the people traveling with you, plan it, exercise moderation, and turn your e-mail or phone off afterwards. All useful tips, but there's one thing you should consider first, though: when is working while on vacation genuinely fun and useful?

It's tempting to take a moment to e-mail a colleague or trouble-shoot. But do you really need to? Shouldn't you simply have arranged things better before leaving? Working on your travels can take a different approach. Vacations give you a great opportunity to focus on things that are easily put off till *mañana* but do matter for your success and work enjoyment in the longer term. Call it inspiration, reflection, or rejuvenation – vacations are well suited to this slower side of your work, because you aren't distracted by... well, your work. Be honest: your office isn't where new ideas generally pop into your head.

HOLIDAYS AND WORK CAN GO WELL TOGETHER, THOUGH HARDLY ANYONE BELIEVES YOU SHOULD ACTUALLY WANT THEM TO.

GREAT VACATIONS ARE FANTASTIC, BUT HAVING CHALLENGING WORK MATTERS MORE.

Great vacations are fantastic, but having challenging work matters more. So spend a little time while traveling to think about (say) that crazy idea for a new product that's been bugging you for a while. Consider going about your work differently. Study the latest research, or think about what you'd change in your work if it was down to you. Keep it unforced and simple: creativity and passion matter more than the details. You can fix that back home. You won't be the first person whose holiday has been the catalyst for something new.

Do we all have to go on vacation at the same time? Try working through the usual holiday weeks and plan your trip for some other time. It's easier to work when everyone else is away. Your supervisor isn't bothering you, your commute isn't gridlocked, the atmosphere's relaxed and you have time for other things. That's working during the vacations too – just not your own.

BEYOND
THE KITSCH

Model Eiffel Towers from France and Brandenburg Gates from Germany, matryoshkas from Russia, and Statues of Liberty from New York: the tourism industry still believes firmly in throw-away kitsch souvenirs. Most of us have by now outgrown the miniature figurines, fridge magnets, mugs with 'I ♥ Wherever' and other tat that ironically often turns out to have been made in China or Bangladesh. They remind us of a time gone by, when travel was more exclusive. But don't underestimate the importance of a souvenir (it's French for *memory*). Or, as the author Ashleigh Brilliant recommends, "Keep some souvenirs of your past, or how will you ever prove it wasn't all a dream?" Always put souvenirs on view, on a bedside table or windowsill, because they're essential for keeping your travel memories alive and letting you enjoy them for longer.

What makes a good souvenir? If there's one key rule of thumb, it's to pick things that aren't meant to be souvenirs. Everyday local products in particular can encapsulate something that a tourist finds unusual, often because they look just that bit different or work a little differently to what you get at home. It turns the humdrum into

the special. Handmade ceramic coasters from Portugal or a rare succulent potted plant from Scandinavia can trigger good memories for years. Look through your house before you leave for things you need, so you know what to buy while away.

Edible souvenirs rarely go wrong. Popular local candies, cookies or other snacks are cheap and easy to buy at the neighborhood supermarket (see tip 15). Mother Nature however may well provide the best souvenirs: unusual flowers, twigs, sand, stones or insects are all free and often available in abundance. Items that are commonplace and considered normal in the destination country, but turn out to be exotic back at home. Be creative in what you bring back: a eucalyptus branch in the bathroom, a selection of mosses for the windowsill or a dead beetle for the bathroom mirror.

The smallest details can at times be crucial for your memories. Try buying an attractive memory box while on holiday and putting together your own mini collection of (say) twigs from the park, a candy wrapper, a hotel soap and the receipt for a memorable meal. If you can enjoy the reminders, you'll enjoy your vacation twice over.

REAL-LIFE ADVENTURES

There are those who think a hotel without room service is roughing it. Others get their kicks from African safaris or Norwegian survival trips. →

For most of us, though, the adventure of a vacation is in the brief adrenalin rush of attractions: climbing a tower, a roller coaster ride or a walk through a dark cave or a city's sewers.

Let's be honest: many of our travel adventures are really fairly predictable experiences. Pre-packaged, if you like. Even a husky dog ride through Lapland is essentially not much more than a sleigh ride over the tundra. Cold, to be sure, and splendidly inspirational – but not exactly daring. Real adventures are found in unpredictability, in extremes. That's why getting lost in a foreign country seems more exciting than a roller coaster.

Abroad, everyday life offers you enough opportunities for adventure. Why not simply by take a look behind the scenes at mundane jobs (see right)? You have to think up these kinds of real-life adventures yourself; life isn't a package tour. There's no guarantee of success either, but asking nicely, humor, and genuine interest can get you a long way. As can courage and inventiveness. Too adventurous for many, but the rewards can be huge. Are you in?

MANY OF OUR TRAVEL ADVENTURES ARE REALLY FAIRLY PREDICTABLE EXPERIENCES.

RIDING THE GARBAGE TRUCK

Garbage trucks go all over the city, handle the weirdest trash and are often manned by peculiar characters who have plenty of opinions and don't suffer fools gladly. Ask a driver if you can hitch a ride on his shift. It's a unique way of learning about your holiday destination. You're sure to meet someone who will have lots of entertaining things to say and you'll learn a bit about a fascinating job at the bottom end of the labor market.

NEXT TO THE CARILLON PLAYER

He's often on his own at the top of a tower, has an unparalleled view of the city, and has a rare and historic job. Try asking if you can go up top with the carillon player: be ready to be amazed at his workplace, learn about the carillon, and let him explain everything you can see. Take coffee and a cake to help convince him and there's every chance you'll get a memorable 'working visit' – even if campanology isn't your thing.

EARLY MORNING BAKERY

The smell of freshly-baked bread, the expert handiwork of the bakers, the heat from the ovens, the repartee among the staff – an early dawn visit to a bakery hard at work can be an impressive experience for all your senses. Ask a baker whether you can watch them work in the morning, and pay double for the freshly baked rolls as a thank-you.

MEETING A CITY

You undoubtedly know the sensation: you arrive one evening in a city you've never been to before and you feel just a touch uncomfortable next morning at breakfast. You don't know which neighborhood you're in, how the city fits together and what it's like on the streets. What you need is an overview, an impression of the city as a whole. But you just don't know how. Instead you leave for the first of the must-sees on your list. As you hop from one attraction to the next, you form an image of the city, gradually and imperfectly.

On vacation, we tend to reduce cities to a set of sights plus what we coincidentally come across in between. We don't do the cities justice then: they're actually extended *Gesamtwerke* that you have to crisscross to appreciate. On top of that, you only have one chance to get a first impression. Your initial acquaintance with a city generally makes the biggest impact on you. You're new, ready to be amazed by anything: the *élan* of the residents, local driving habits, impressive historic façades or even something as tiny as a neatly depicted human figure in the crosswalk lights. It's a shame not to revel in that moment. That's why you should always plan your first date with a city carefully.

There's a great way to get to know a city initially, and it's called public transport. Not a hop-on, hop-off sightseeing bus, whose action radius goes no further than a few tourist highlights. Instead, take a regular bus or tram service to the end of the line and back.

Sitting by the window, you can observe the entire city at a comfortable pace, with enough stops for you to be able to absorb it all. Take one of the longer routes, one that crosses the whole city. It will show you a nice cross-section of the place, from center to outer suburbs. And if you go past interesting sights, make a note of the stops so that you can get out on the way back.

If public transport isn't your thing, cabs are just as good for that first inspiring encounter with the city. Ask your driver for the ultimate round trip to get to know the city. It'll cost more than a bus ticket, but with more opportunities to get exactly what you want. Tell your driver what you're interested in and he'll adapt the route to suit. Gliding through the streets with a local music station in the background, you may immediately experience one of your happiest moments in the new city.

SUPERMARKET SAFARI

"A person buying ordinary products in a supermarket is in touch with his deepest emotions," observed the economist Kenneth Galbraith once astutely. At home we often see supermarkets as a necessary evil, but it's different when we're away. Supermarkets abroad are a cultural destination *par excellence*. Stroll past the shelves like a museum visitor and you'll get an enjoyable impression of a country's (culinary) culture.

Market halls, butchers, wineries, and farmers' markets: food retail outlets come in many guises. But on vacation it's the bigger everyday supermarkets – a Carrefour in France, a Trader Joe's in California – that are the most interesting to visit. First and foremost, it's about the local favorites. Spanish supermarkets are an ode to canned sardines, tuna, and mackerel. Japanese supermarkets are known for their candy, from traditional Japanese caramels and lychee gummy bears to KitKats in every conceivable flavor. The packaging and brand names are often amusing, from the splendid cool minimalism of Finnish salted licorice to toilet paper called *Happy End* in German supermarkets. It makes supermarkets the ideal places to find amusing or regional gifts (see tip 12).

If you want to know what the local residents' daily staples are, or the regional dishes, look for the deli (most supermarkets have one now), where you can find locally produced goods. And why not pick out some nice local cheese, sausage, or a salad for a picnic in the park? Or stock up for the evening meal. After a whole day sightseeing and snacking, making your own version of a local specialty can be a welcome and active challenge.

"The grocery store is the great equalizer where mankind comes to grips with the facts of life like toilet tissue," said a store owner philosophically once. Grocery shopping has become such a shared part of human experience that the supermarket has come to symbolize everyday life. Whether it's newlyweds, or a mom with her toddler, or an old grandad, you see authentic people in the supermarket, in their everyday splendor buying everyday products. People-watching is another reason why a supermarket safari is a must. For you, the observant tourist, other people's everyday routine will hold entertaining and exceptional revelations.

WE TRY HARDER

The glorious leading roles in our vacations go to the capitals, as if they're the screen stars who are the sexiest and the most talented. From Tokyo and London to Paris and Beijing, we ooh and aah *en masse* at the iconic sights of these so-called first cities. Biggest is best, right? →

The dominance of 'alpha cities' in tourism doesn't exactly come from left field: most are endowed with a wealth of museums, attractions, and other tourist goodies. But their pulling power also comes from their image. First-city marketeers work assiduously to raise our expectations of a stay in their metropolis, with smooth words and pretty pictures. Many first cities are however finding it more and more difficult to maintain that promise of being the ultimate holiday destination. Mass tourism and other effects of globalization mean that many are plagued by a mix of gentrification, congestion, and pollution. On top of that, they have gotten used to being popular. Services in many first cities are under pressure: long queues, full hotels, tourist traps, overpriced restaurants, discourteous staff – how long do we put up with it for? Here come the second cities.

In the shadow of their show-stopping colleagues, second cities remain under the radar for many of us. Think of Yokohama instead of Tokyo, Marseille instead of Paris, Ankara instead of Istanbul, Rotterdam instead of Amsterdam and perhaps (before too long) Brooklyn rather than Manhattan. Second cities might be the second largest, but not always the second best. Many are a bit unusual, though it may be hard to put your finger on why. But most of all, they're generally hospitable and ambitious. Avis, the second-largest car rental company, used the slogan "We Try Harder" successfully for years, and with good reason.

What makes a second city special? "Second cities are often a dialed-down, rough-around-the-edges, more genuine representation of a nation's way of life," says the travel journalist Oliver Smith. Away from the

IN THE SHADOW OF THEIR SHOW-STOPPING COLLEAGUES, SECOND CITIES REMAIN UNDER THE RADAR FOR MANY OF US.

AWAY FROM THE TOURIST PRESSURE AND HUBBUB, SECOND CITIES ALLOW A MUCH MORE PLEASANT, HONEST, AND AUTHENTIC EXPERIENCE.

tourist pressure and hubbub, they allow a much more pleasant, honest, and authentic experience. Interestingly, many second cities are ports: essential in the global distribution not only of goods but also of ideas, culture, and architecture. Precisely because they're distinct from the capital, second cities are often more creative and more daring. "Why did the gay movement get going in San Francisco? Why did house music happen in Detroit? Outsider status, a sense of independence through neglect – these are better spurs to action than life at the very center of things," according to the journalist Janan Ganesh.

Skipping the Londons and New Yorks, and with them many of a country's alleged must-sees, demands courage and a different agenda, because it's not as if second cities fall short in terms of character and sights to see. Inevitably, second cities draw visitors who, like their destinations themselves, know that size doesn't matter and like to do things differently. Are you in?

SMELLING MEMORIES

Mimicking the aroma of sunscreen and sea air, a dab of this oil on your pulse points serves as a quick escape. Shut your eyes, take a sniff, and imagine that the office's fluorescent lights are actually the sun's rays.
– Beauty Editor Marianne Mychaskiw about the Urban Decay Go Naked Perfume Oil

Vacation destinations provide inspiration to many perfume makers. Fleur de Portofino, for instance, with a mix of Sicilian lemon, jasmine, and violet leaf presents itself as "a Mediterranean getaway". Or Big Sur Coastline, with scents of salt air, camphor, and foggy chaparral, "will transport you to your last road trip down California's coastal Highway 1".

What makes vacation destinations smell so inspirational? Is it the unique local aromas hanging in the air, in the woods, by the sea, or at the market? Probably, but it's just as important that these holiday scents get inseparably associated with the freedom and adventure that you're experiencing during your trip. The olfactory sense is the only one directly linked to the brain – in fact to the same areas that our emotions come from, the amygdala and hippocampus. Smells therefore create our longest-lasting memories and even evoke more powerful emotions than sounds, images or words.

So your nose is your strongest memory. People who know that fact allow for it: the stronger your vacation memories, the longer and more intense your later enjoyment of it at home will be. A holiday scent now often nestles subconsciously in our minds, particularly if we were exposed to a particular aroma a lot on the spot – take the lavender fields in France, for instance. But smells should actually have a special status in your trip, as a permanent item on your to-do list.

Powerful, aromatic memories of vacations are created by deliberately scouting local scents and breathing them in deeply on your travels. Alertness and inventiveness will take you a long way. Buy aromatic candies or snacks from a local supermarket and eat one every afternoon. Put a bag of local herbs in your car or your bag. Buy an unusual local flower at the market and leave it to dry in your hotel room. Choose less obvious aromas too: keep the serviette in Spain that you wiped your fingers on after a paella, or a T-shirt that went to the laundry in India. Take the most striking aromas back home and you will be amazed how your nose manages to conjure memories up again in a flash, years later. Oh, that smell – I remember it exactly!

A BETTER TOURIST

Good food and drink, pleasant excursions, long sessions lazing in the sun – pleasure and enjoyment are the ultimate aim of a vacation for many. The experienced hedonist prefers leaving principles and problems at home. Even so, there's such a thing as Relative Hedonism.
It presupposes that there is an enjoyment aspect to Good, that charitable work can be pleasurable. Not that there's anything wrong with unashamed fun, but it can quickly become egocentric and superficial. There can be more to life on vacation too.

Charitable tourism, the idea of getting satisfaction from doing something philanthropic while away, isn't something many people have in their mind's eye. We seem to be too busy with our own pleasure. Be aware however that locals in many holiday destinations are less well off than you and have to work very hard. Your entertainment is often their livelihood.

Vacations are the perfect moment to do good and to feel good about it. It's when you've got the time. You don't have to start with something grandiose: charity can start small, like paying attention to others and appreciating them. The doorman, waiter or cleaner all help make your vacation more fun and will surely appreciate a chat or a thank-you. Or you can take small souvenirs from your own country – traditional cookies for instance – that you can leave as thanks.

If you want, you can devote your whole vacation to voluntary work: everything from plowing the land to building schools and teaching, often in developing countries. Being a 'voluntourist' is a bridge too far for most, however, but it doesn't mean your trip has to be a philanthropy-free zone. With a little effort, doing good can be made to fit in well with a regular vacation. Contact a reputable local charity while planning your journey and ask if there are ongoing efforts you can get involved in during your trip – handing out food parcels, for instance. Make donations at your destination to good causes that you come across (or search out). Anything from churches to museums or playgrounds. Offer a homeless person a cup of coffee or a sandwich, take time for a good chat with that elderly guy on a park bench (see tip 8). Hotel chains are increasingly often offering community-based volunteer opportunities to let their guests do something in return. If they don't, simply ask them for suggestions for what you could do in return locally; after all, they know the area.

Your own creativity and decisiveness make it perfectly possible to do good things during your trip. This will make you a better tourist. And, it also offers welcome variation in your vacation days, undoubtedly otherwise full of fun and consumerism. In other words, doing good will also do your trip good.

PERFECT STRANGERS IN A CAPSULE

Hail a taxi cab, open the door to a burst of easy listening music, breathe in the poppy air freshener, lean over the seat, and say hello to the next Jean-Paul Sartre or Kahlil Gibran.
– Risa Mickenberg, writer

It's easy to treat cab drivers as a necessary evil for getting you from A to B, but that's not doing them justice. All over the globe, taxi drivers are a priceless source of information and worldly wisdom. Most of them have known their area long enough to give you up-to-date and surprising tips. So always ask what's new in town and find out what their personal favorites are. Get them to say what living in the city is like and the chat will get more substantial before you know it. After all, a cabbie knows more than just the roads. They'll have an opinion on a range of hot issues and know (thanks to their unerring sense of direction?) everything about the right path through life.

The capsule in which you and your driver are moving is the ultimate setting for a dialog, according to Manjo van Boxtel, who drives a cab herself. She points out that you and your driver don't have each other's undivided attention, and neither does the chat. You can flit between subjects, there's always a way out and in fact that makes sharing personal thoughts easier. Silences are often awkward in a conversation, but much less so in a taxi – after all, you're both looking out. You're physically close together, which helps the chat get more personal, yet you hardly see each other. If you're no longer enjoying the conversation, you can shut up shop simply enough. That lack of obligation means you don't need a verbal suit of armor: you're in control of what's said.

When you're on vacation, uninhibited chats with the locals are often valuable, but rare. All the more reason to grab a cab more often on your travels. Not all cab drivers are eloquent philosophers, of course. Don't forget that their job can be unpredictable and risky. Weirdos, clowns, douchebags, eccentrics, and egos: taxi drivers share their workplace with the strangest people. It can make them understandably cautious or quirky at times. But that unpredictable, idiosyncratic trait is precisely the attraction. It can be a thin line between madman and genius – for cab drivers too.

FESTIVE RITUALS

What's the best way to get to know a country? Where's the best place to experience local everyday life? Those are typical questions that the ambitious tourist may ask. After the umpteenth attraction, museum or shopping street, you want something different. Something real, about normal people. →

You can visit museums that tell you about the local culture, of course. You can walk through neighborhoods to catch a glimpse of the locals' everyday existence. If you want to get a deeper taste of a society, though, you can instead go looking for a country's festivals. It is pretty simple, though not many tourists realize it, for a curious outsider to join in with the celebrations of the local populace.

A graduation ceremony, a baptism, or a wedding – pivotal moments in human lives that we often celebrate. Many of these gatherings are public and you can simply join in, even if you are a tourist. It is amusing and educational to discover how people elsewhere in the world perceive those universal moments that you commemorate at home too. There are limits at times to how public the events are, but that doesn't have to spoil the fun. When you're abroad, simply watching the bride and groom arrive and depart can even be inspirational.

Sports are perhaps the most widely accessible 'festivities' that you can attend as a vacationer. They are rarely on tourists' to-do lists, but going to a local ball game offers entertaining insights into how the townsfolk pass their time. In particular when popular local clubs are involved, sporting

AFTER THE UMPTEENTH ATTRACTION, MUSEUM OR SHOPPING STREET, YOU WANT SOMETHING DIFFERENT.

IT IS PRETTY SIMPLE FOR A CURIOUS OUTSIDER TO JOIN IN WITH THE CELEBRATIONS OF THE LOCAL POPULACE.

events become local rituals, saturated with culture and passion. Find out what derby matches there are and see if you can get hold of a ticket. Popular sports such as soccer in Brazil, baseball in America or cricket in India are must-sees for tourists aware enough to realize that the amusements of the local populace are sights worth seeing in their own right.

Party gear, parades and street markets make national public holidays perhaps the best rituals to get involved in when you're a tourist. Parties like Koningsdag in the Netherlands, the Oktoberfest in Germany, Saint Patrick's Day in Ireland or Halloween in America give you an authentic glimpse of how a country celebrates its traditions. They'll often catch you by surprise, because as a tourist you don't know the local events calendar. So look it up beforehand and make sure that you know where and when the party fun is worth catching.

Attending a local festivity can be a welcome change to your stops at museums, monuments, and other sights. The festive rituals may sometimes scarcely differ from what you would do back home – a comforting observation, or even a delightful sense of familiarity. More often however, the differences are substantial. It may feel as if you have lifted the corner of the veil and seen the country's soul.

GOLD IN THE MUD

In many ways, a visit to a metropolis is not so different from going to an amusement park. Both offer an abundance of noise, spectacle, consumables, and visitors, in queues or otherwise. You leave a fun park after an afternoon, though, whereas you'll hang around longer as a city tourist. You need a chance to recover if you're going to keep that up.

You mostly rest in the evening in your hotel, exhausted. But particularly in a city, a bit of restfulness during the daytime is a great element to include in the day's program too. A carefully chosen, serene spot gives you respite from the urban chaos. It lets you enjoy an unhurried coffee, read a good book, and recharge your batteries. The contrast with the urban hustle and bustle and with your undoubtedly packed program makes peace and quiet in the city an intense experience. Like finding a nugget of gold in the mud.

Peace and quiet in the city seem rarer than they actually are. Cemeteries, which are worth visiting anyway when abroad, are sure to be restful, as are botanical gardens. Hotel lobbies can be wonderfully serene too. And comfortable, particularly between midday and 3 p.m. when the cleaners have just left and the new guests have yet to arrive. Some hotels also have rooftop terraces that are surprisingly empty during the day. The higher, the calmer.

Once you've developed a nose for it, or learned you should always ask, there are lots of nice quiet places to be found in any city. They range from small cafes with no music where time seems to stand still, to small historic museums with amateurish but cozy coffee corners. Perhaps the nicest (and best hidden) oases of silence are courtyard gardens. Especially in historic city centers, the inner courtyards of residential blocks are often beautifully green and serene, with benches and perhaps the distant sound of someone playing a piano. Some of these courtyard gardens are publicly accessible, but quite often only through an insignificant little door that you have to know about. So ask! It makes the discovery even more special, of course.

Madrid once issued a free brochure giving the best spots for enjoying its wonderful sunsets. After all, what's more enjoyable than an afternoon on a hillside or roof patio, drinking in the air and watching the buildings change color? Sometimes the city is like a fun park; getting your breath back makes you a better visitor.

OUT ON THE EDGE

Many of us see cities like a fried egg, or at least that's what it looks like from above: sunny side up, with the yolk the place where it all happens. But there are others, gourmets, who know that the tastiest part of a fried egg is the outside edge, crispy and a touch greasy. →

THE RADIUS OF ACTION IN OUR CITY VACATIONS IS GENERALLY LIMITED TO A SMALL ZONE WHERE THE SIGHTS ARE CONCENTRATED: THE CITY CENTER.

The radius of action in our city vacations is generally limited to a small zone where the sights are concentrated: the city center. That's a pity, because the outskirts of the city are just as worth seeing, in their own way. Urban peripheries are places where special and exciting things happen. The pioneers and others who have set up shop here often do work that is so large-scale, idiosyncratic or plain dirty that the prim and pricey city center isn't even close to being an option.

Ports and industrial zones in particular are fascinating fringes. In among the industry you'll find artists, designers, entrepreneurs, and cowboy operators. They run their studios, factories or workshops in old and frequently stunning factory premises where you can often just walk in for a chat. Their presence creates a whimsical, fascinating mix of creativity and industriousness that quickly makes a visit to the area an adventure of discovery. A quirky seafood restaurant or an alternative nightclub in an old warehouse: some eateries and entertainment venues deliberately make you come to the periphery. They know that the trip and the search are half the fun.

Green belts around cities have their temptations too, in a different way. You see trees, grass, and water there instead of glass, steel, and concrete. Emerging gradually sometimes, with expanses of no man's land between, or with knife-edge transitions where apartment blocks are juxtaposed with meadows or woodland. You can even be in the city and spot hares, water birds, or other wild animals: the ultimate confrontation between wild and civilized. Environmentally conscious cities often have surrounding green belts that are home to wind turbines, urban agriculture, or organic farmers' markets, where you can witness a new eco-friendly future arising.

The periphery is also the literal and figurative margin of a complex society, where cities put their homeless people and other traveling folk . So as well as being adventurous, the urban edge may show the inevitable, less cheerful side of city life. Beauty and the beast: that duality helps

make the urban periphery so fascinating. It means that these are excellent areas for seasoned tourists, those who can appreciate the full splendor and intense dreariness of life on the fringes.

"I want to stand as close to the edge as I can without going over. Out on the edge you see all kinds of things you can't see from the center," said the writer Kurt Vonnegut. So, forget the center for a while and go for the crispness and flavor at the edges. Study the map carefully beforehand. Or the best approach is perhaps to find someone who knows the city and will tell you exactly where to go. Or will even accompany you, because the city limits are often also the boundary of your comfort zone.

SOME DELIBERATELY MAKE YOU COME TO THE PERIPHERY. THEY KNOW THAT THE TRIP AND THE SEARCH ARE HALF THE FUN.

GO RESIDENTIAL

Where is the best place to learn about the Netherlands: the Rijksmuseum or an Amsterdam suburb like IJburg? What tells you more about San Francisco, Alcatraz or Los Altos? And where can you find the real Rio de Janeiro: the statue of Christ the Redeemer, or the hill slopes with the favelas? If you want to get to know a city or country better, look for the everyday life. Whether that's rigidly designed new towns in the Netherlands, nostalgic suburbs in America or lively ghettoes in Brazil, an afternoon spent there often tells you more than a whole bunch of tourist attractions.

Strolling through picturesque city districts is always nice, but real everyday life is often found elsewhere. It is more likely to be manifest outside the center, at the end of the metro line, in residential areas where people like you and me – most of the population – live out their lives. There are no cutesy stores and spectacular sights there.

A neighborhood safari is a welcome change in your trek past the tourist magnets. It's not about finding entertainment in highlights: it shows you what life is like for the vast majority. Residential areas offer simple and recognizable pleasures: what's more entertaining than watching the local kids playing,

seeing the clean washing on the line and looking on as someone builds a rabbit hutch? People's lives elsewhere can be reassuringly similar to your own, or inspirationally different – hey, look at how the milkman still delivers to the door here!

From a tourist perspective, the everyday side of residential districts abroad is often amusing and educational. But be aware that not everything is equally worth a visit. The most interesting neighborhoods are the ones with daring architecture, built with clearly stated ideas about 'how to live'. How can you find them? Go for it: phone a local architect's office and ask where you should go.

If this sounds a bit tedious, remember residential areas have their attractions too. Such as the absurd, master-planned Sun City in California, where only the elderly live. Or the VM houses in Copenhagen, with spectacular pointed balconies inspired by the film *Titanic*, where the residents can mimic Leonardo di Caprio: "I'm flying!" Almost every city has an iconic residential district, or at least an unusual one. Go find them, walk around and give your eyes a treat. There's every chance of this excursion sticking longer in the memory than the brief adrenalin hit of tourist attractions.

THERE ARE OTHERS HERE WITH US

"Why do tourists hate other tourists?" It was a pretty straight-forward question from a middle-aged Burmese who we met at a small pagoda in Bagan. He was curious why we'd asked which temple wouldn't have a lot of 'foreigners' at sunset. To him, our desire to avoid others seemed crazy. We tried to think of a way to describe our particular mindset to him, but we struggled to come up with a logical answer to his simple question.

– Alesha and Jarryd, travel writers →

It's striking just how often the tempting ads of vacation destinations don't show tourists. With a few exceptions (theme parks, beaches and festivals), we clearly don't view the prospect of other visitors as attractive, according to the travel industry at any rate. You see the same thing in our own holiday snaps however. We're often happy to wait a moment to take them until all the other tourists are out of the way. As if we were utterly alone.

When we're on vacation, our relationship with other travelers is odd: we often seem to avoid people who are doing the same thing as us, or we pretend they aren't there. Just watch how little contact there is between tourists, even at sights where everybody ends up squashed into each other's personal space. That doesn't necessarily have to mean that tourists are bothered by each other, though. "In many tourist situations with shared goals, when people have come to see and experience the same features and activities, the tolerance for fellow visitors may be quite high," says Philip Pearce in his book Tourist Behaviour.

Even so, the rise of mass tourism seems to have driven tourist numbers at many destinations beyond people's tolerance. Residents of popular tourist cities such as Barcelona and Amsterdam have been expressing their disquiet for some years. Tourists themselves also seem to be increasingly aware of each other. New travel books such as Not For Tourists or How to Avoid the Other Tourists are the writing on the wall. If you're someone who likes avoiding other travelers, you've probably already got a few strategies: seeing the sights early morning before the crowds, or late in the evening, finding quieter local spots during the day and gathering tips from insiders beforehand that for instance tell you about the entrances that only the locals know.

ISN'T IT HYPOCRITICAL TO WANT TO AVOID TOURISTS WHEN YOU'RE ACTUALLY ONE YOURSELF?

YOU MAY WANT LIVELY CONTACTS WITH THE LOCAL POPULACE, BUT IN MANY PLACES YOU'LL SPEND MORE TIME IN THE VICINITY OF OTHER TOURISTS.

Isn't it hypocritical to want to avoid tourists when you're actually one yourself? It's obvious that you might dislike seeing too many people or want to avoid crowded situations that look too touristy. But wanting to dodge other travelers altogether, so that it's just you and the locals, would seem to be an unhealthy and unrealistic overreaction. As much as you may want lively contacts with the local populace, in many places it's very likely that you'll spend more time in the vicinity of other tourists. Researchers tell us that direct and personal encounters with fellow tourists are moreover seen as positive more often than indirect encounters. On top of that, various studies support the notion that personal contacts with strangers reduce stereotypical prejudices and foster positive attitudes. In other words, other tourists are not only an inevitable aspect of your vacation, but they are also in fact an opportunity to make become a better tourist.

THE MERE EXPOSURE EFFECT

No matter how much other countries can tempt us as tourists, we often check them off mercilessly afterwards: been there, done that. After all, vacations are all about the new and the unfamiliar. Why revisit places you've already been? →

DRAWN BY THE PROMISE OF THE UNKNOWN, WE SPEND MOST OF OUR HOLIDAY TIME VISITING NEW DESTINATIONS.

Drawn by the promise of the unknown, we spend most of our holiday time visiting new destinations. That may feel enterprising, as if you're a true world traveler, but it ignores the power of repetition. The second visit to a city or country is almost always better. Returning to where you've been before gives a certain pleasure and reassurance. Or, according to the author Tyler Moss, "The streets and subway seem easier to navigate; previously patronized restaurants and bars feel like old friends." It's what scientists call the *mere exposure effect*: we value a city or country more highly once we've gotten to know it.

Our style of vacationing enhances the mere exposure effect. Driven by the fear of missing out, we tend to check off as many of the must-sees as possible for each new destination. We behave differently on a return visit, though, because you now know the essentials and so you relax and take more time. You look beyond the must-sees for your entertainment and discover the nice-to-dos: from a picturesque little neighborhood or a historic house museum to a bustling market hall or a new, modern city park. They may be smaller and less well known, but often more authentic and less touristy. It makes you more likely to feel they're a special discovery.

There are people who fly to the same spot every year all their lives, like migratory birds. They seem to have developed a faculty to enjoy missing out. Nevertheless, there's something to be said for visiting a city or country more regularly. It's the only way to watch what happens over the years, seeing old working-class districts flourish, noting the effect of a new tram line, or seeing new generations of immigrants open new stores and restaurants. That perspective on change – often lacking in your home country because you're in the middle of it all – is at least as valuable as random snapshots from around the world. On top of that, you'll notice that it's not only your destination that changes: you do too. The sights that drew you as a student aren't what will charm you three decades later. "No man ever steps in the same river twice, for it's not the same river and he's not the same man," says the philosopher Heraclitus.

So why not try a return visit a little more often when picking your next travel destinations? You can turn it round too at new destinations by acting more as if you've been there before. The next time you're new in town, just act like you're at home: relax, take your time and start with the nice-to-dos. The essentials will come later. Or perhaps never at all, because there are good holidays without must-sees too.

WE BEHAVE DIFFERENTLY ON A RETURN VISIT. YOU NOW KNOW THE ESSENTIALS AND SO YOU RELAX AND TAKE MORE TIME.

A HEROIC ACT OF WILLPOWER

If you deliberately try to get the max from your vacation, you're bound to hit the issue of "enough is enough." How full should you plan your days? Moderation is awkward. Many of us suffer to some extent from *horror vacui* (Latin for fear of emptiness), a condition 'discovered' by artists who did not dare to leave any empty spaces in their works. →

"The problem of the western world is that people stuff their vacations full of activities, as if they're afraid of doing nothing," says the philosopher and businessman Govert Derix. It's true: traveling has become more hectic and more 'productive.' Ever more exotic destinations, cultural immersion and adventure activities, with diversions in the meantime via digital media. Derix makes the case for a political Vacationers' Party, a counter-movement fighting for *amor vacui* (love of emptiness) and promoting proper holidaying as being essential for our civilization.

Doing nothing relaxes you. According to research, the only vacationers who feel happier after their trip are those who said they felt "very relaxed" on their vacation. But there's still a question of how much of doing nothing is enough? Are we talking about taking an occasional time out,

deliberately enjoying the moment? Or about lying for days on the beach or in alpine meadows with a big stack of books and music, or someone to chew the fat with?

There is also another, more advanced form of doing nothing. One where the 'content junkie' in you goes cold turkey and avoids all input – no books, no smartphone music, nobody to chat to. Where you go looking for peace, inner calm, letting all your thoughts and feelings ebb away and trying to achieve a deeper level of consciousness. Or, in the words of the philosopher Mortimer Adler, "You have to allow a certain amount of time in which you are doing nothing in order to have things occur to you, to let your mind think."

That may sound woolier than it is. Look at it this way: the contrast with your daily life is what makes a vacation valuable. If that life

IF YOUR LIFE IS ALREADY RICHLY FILLED AND ONLY GETTING BUSIER, WHY SHOULD YOU DO THE SAME WHEN HOLIDAYING?

INSTEAD OF FLINGING YOURSELF HEADLONG INTO ANOTHER EXCITING ADVENTURE, TRY HEADING IN THE OPPOSITE DIRECTION FOR ONCE.

is already richly filled and only getting busier, why should you do the same when holidaying? Our vacations are the only moments when we can do nothing for days at a time, to experience what that emptiness feels like. This will start feeling like a more attractive prospect at some point if you've already got lots of ambitious trips under your belt. Instead of flinging yourself headlong into another exciting adventure, try heading in the opposite direction for once.

A successful do-nothing vacation does not necessarily require an organized quiet retreat in a monastery. You can do it yourself if properly prepared – read up about mindfulness first. Find a quiet and simple spot, a mountain cabin or holiday cottage, where you can spend several days or preferably a week and hardly have to do anything. Avoid news, books, music, social media, television and other stimuli. Instead, adopt a clear daily routine of straightforward meals, plenty of sleep and exercise, and contemplating the future for long periods each day.

Sitting still for an hour or two feels like a heroic act of willpower at first. Treat it as a skill that you have to acquire, taking the knocks along the way. If you succeed, you'll find deeper layers of recall within yourself as you go, where lost memories, new ideas, and wise insights slumber, along with unsuspected ambitions and emotions that need closure. Discovering them can have quite an impact, so that your period of silence is still fruitful. Refreshed and enriched, you will return home with ideas and insights that will prove their worth over the years. Doing nothing was never so rewarding.

MENTAL SOUVENIRS

You may not always realize it, but there are lots of learning moments hidden in vacations. Packing your bags before you set off is already forcing you to prioritize. Then the airports in many exotic vacation spots, where getting a taxi is a lesson in firm negotiation. And the familiar issue of accepting – sigh! – that going with the flow works better in many leisure destinations than the regimented timetable you use at home. Treat lessons and insights like these as the mental souvenirs of your vacation. And cherish them. →

YOU MAY FIND THAT YOUR VACATION IS LIKE A PERSONAL COACH HELPING WITH YOUR WORRIES AND AMBITIONS.

You may even find that your vacation is like a personal coach helping with your worries and ambitions. What do you want from your work? What could make your relationship better? What do you dream of? Far away from the latest fads, you may find answers to the questions in your life, both large and small. Which doesn't mean that you can order them as simply as a drink on the patio... Gaining new insights about your work, happiness or other big themes in your life while traveling takes practice and patience. That's vacationing for experts.

What can you do to make sure you come back home with more than just nice memories and snapshots? A modest three-part recommendation:

BEFORE

Pack your mental bags too. Think about what you want from your vacation. Write down a couple of key questions or challenges and stick it as a reminder on the inside of your suitcase or on your toiletries bag. They'll travel with you and nestle in the back of your mind.

DURING

An unusual chat with an old woman in the park, a creatively furnished hotel, the dedication of a baker – you'll find plenty to be amazed at on vacation. The subjects are up to you, but your experience is often linked to what's happening in your life at that moment. Write down your observations, associations, and experiences, big or small, before they fade.

AFTER

What may seem obvious while you are away can be valuable pieces of the jigsaw back home. You'd normally forget them once you're back in the maelstrom of the working week, but now you've written them down. Read your notes through carefully at the end of the vacation, or when you're back home. Look through them and make connections. The aim now is to embed what you have learned and genuinely do something with it. The best opportunities for change are when you get back from vacation. Or, to paraphrase the writer Richie Norton, "a little piece of everywhere you go, may become a big part of everything you do."

WHAT MAY SEEM OBVIOUS WHILE YOU ARE AWAY CAN BE VALUABLE PIECES OF THE JIGSAW BACK HOME.

BACK TO REALITY

One of the reasons why vacations don't ultimately make you happier, studies reveal, is the stress of starting work again. That tension can even start building up during the final days of your break. You're still trying to enjoy yourself, while already leafing through next week's diary in your mind. Once you're at work, it's amazing how you can have forgotten your vacation entirely after just a few hours on the job. A mailbox bursting at the seams and new deadlines soon sour that lovely relaxed feeling you came home with.

Post-vacation blues, the back home syndrome – at least half of all employees admit it affects them. It's a feeling that's perhaps best expressed in the pop song *Back to Life, Back to Reality*, a persistent mantra that echoes round the mind for some post-vacation blues sufferers. The better the vacation, the deeper the blues, given that they come from the discrepancy between the fun of traveling and the everyday grind. "It's like an anxiety disorder," states the psychologist Erika Martinez. "Symptoms include excessive worry, tiredness, irritability, loss of appetite, strong feelings of nostalgia, headaches, and poor attention or concentration."

Can you fight the post-vacation blues? What helps, at any rate, are more gradual vacation-work transitions, particularly if you are coming home with jetlag or making a sudden switch from 30 Celsius and sunshine to 15 and overcast. So try staying home on the Monday before starting again. Keep hold of the vacation feel for longer, with photos on the fridge door or desk, by telling friends and neighbors about your trip, or by looking through your memory box (see tip 12). For some, the best medicine is to book the next vacation as soon as you're home – something to look forward to!

But wait. Aren't those remedies avoiding the real issue? Post-vacation blues often appear because being back means tackling all the things you left for later. Surely you could organize that better or differently? After all, prevention is better than cure. The key issue is whether you're still satisfied with the work you do. A nice job makes a big difference. 75% of satisfied employees are raring to go again after their vacations; no less than 83% of dissatisfied ones aren't. This suggests post-vacation blues can largely be seen as a 'sickness' afflicting those who feel their work is not rewarding enough. Anyone who gets them badly should therefore – yes, it's not easy – look for more fulfilling work, either in their current job or elsewhere. Some reluctance on the first day back is natural enough, but it shouldn't last long.

ON VACATION, WE TEND TO REDUCE CITIES TO A SET OF SIGHTS PLUS WHAT WE COINCIDENTALLY COME ACROSS IN BETWEEN.

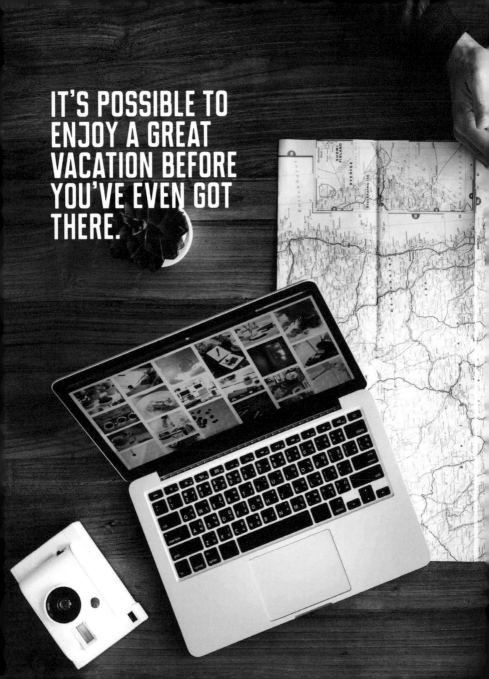

IT'S POSSIBLE TO ENJOY A GREAT VACATION BEFORE YOU'VE EVEN GOT THERE.

THE CAPSULE IN WHICH
YOU AND YOUR DRIVER ARE
MOVING IS THE ULTIMATE
SETTING FOR A DIALOG.

RESIDENTIAL AREAS OFFER SIMPLE AND RECOGNIZABLE PLEASURES, TELLING YOU MORE THAN MANY TOURIST ATTRACTIONS PUT TOGETHER.

SUPERMARKETS ABROAD
ARE A CULTURAL DESTINATION
PAR EXCELLENCE.

READ MORE

The Art of Travel (2003)
Alain de Botton
(Penguin)

"Alain de Botton aims to change the way we travel. Forget about that breathless search for distant thrills, and concentrate on enjoying where you are – even in a motorway café."
—Boyd Tonkin, The Independent

Tourist Behaviour and the Contemporary World (2011)
Philip L. Pearce
(Channel View Publications)

"A remarkably broad and in-depth treatment of the issues shaping the world of tourism today. The book is a must-read for tourism researchers in assessing new and emerging research streams that will make a difference."
—John C. Crotts, College of Charleston

The Lonely Planet Guide to Experimental Travel (2005)
Rachael Antony, Joel Henry
(Lonely Planet)

"Those aching for a relief from packaged tours or Club Med vacations would do well to pick up this ut-of-the-ordinary guide. If nothing else, this unusual book reminds us of the joy of discovery."
—Publishers Weekly

Quiet London (2001)
and other cities in this series
Siobhan Wall
(Frances Lincoln Publishers)

"Full of whispered pleasures, this off-the-beaten-track guide shows you where to sit and stare - Zen gardens, quiet cafes, secret pools, tiny museums, blissful bookshops."
—Sainsbury's Magazine

Waiting for the Weekend (2011)
Witold Rybczynski
(Penguin Books)

"An enchanting, strikingly profound meditation on the relationship between leisure and labor."
—Publishers Weekly

Taxi Driver Wisdom (1996)
Risa Mickenberg
(Chronicle Books)

"A collection of one-liners - insights on love, pleasure, fate and other topics that drivers expounded on from over their shoulders to Mickenberg in the back seat."
—Vincent Barone, amNewYork

HOW TO VISIT

TIPS FOR
A TRULY
REWARDING
VISIT

AN ART

JOHAN
IDEMA

**STOP
WANDERING,
START
ACTING!**

MUSEUM

BIS

HOW TO VISIT AN ART MUSEUM

"The only way to understand art is to go to a museum and look at it," French painter Renoir suggests. But once inside, this is easier said than done. What do you do when the label simply reads *Untitled, 1973*? Where to look when a painting offers you a picturesque yet undisguised view of a giant vagina? And how to react when the museum guard stares at you for far too long?

How to Visit an Art Museum offers fresh perspectives on how to behave once inside a museum. Whether you're a first-timer or a frequent visitor, it shows you the sense and nonsense of museum etiquette. The typical museum behavior – "Walk slowly, but keep walking" – is seldom the most rewarding. That's why this book encourages you to look outside the box and tackle the challenges that art presents to us by taking matters into your own hands.

Find out how you can use museum guards to your advantage. Learn the rules of thumb for distinguishing good from bad art. Explore how kids are able to offer you glimpses of the world that's hidden behind an art-work. *How to Visit an Art Museum* shows you how a little courage and creativity can go a long way to making your museum visit truly worthwhile. Because, ultimately, the art museum is what you make it.

Buy it here: www.bispublishers.com

ACKNOWLEDGEMENTS

Woman walking
Binalfrodo
flickr.com/photos/
bindalfrodo/4879656508

Louvre Museum
prateekb
flickr.com/photos/
prateekb/36724797342/in/
album-72157688283820415

Trevi fountain
Grant Bishop
flickr.com/photos/64609422@
N04/5964426773

Eiffel Tower souvenirs
Vinicius Pinheiro
flickr.com/photos/vineco/4302988036

Tourism kills the city
Khairil Yusof
flickr.com/photos/57634952@
N00/27100635471

People taking pictures
Clemens v. Vogelsang
flickr.com/photos/
vauvau/11775239636/in/photostream

Cruise ship with tourists
Julien Belli
flickr.com/photos/
julienbelli/30026459143

1. The Perfect Holistay
   Marius Lengwiler
   flickr.com/photos/
   mle86/4939351988

2. Pre-Vacation Happiness
   rawpixel.com/image/8657

3. Sick On Arrival
   Kate Brady
   flickr.com/photos/cliche/12005045

4. Rent A German
   Visit Grand Island
   flickr.com/photos/
   greatergrandisland/20507517442

5. Bad Stuff Is Going To Happen
   Daniel Lobo
   flickr.com/photos/
   daquellamanera/293848920

6. The Princes Of Serendip
   Franck Michel
   flickr.com/photos/
   franckmichel/8056893482

7. Future Memories
   Stig Nygaard
   flickr.com/photos/
   stignygaard/6035942305

8. Small Talk, Big Impact
   Gareth Williams
   flickr.com/photos/
   gareth1953/9247485727/in/
   photostream

9. To Airbnb Or Not To Airbnb?
   Alper Çuğun
   flickr.com/photos/
   alper/28791618636/in/photolist-
   KSdz8S-oTLpLF

10. A Day Alone
    Franck Michel
    flickr.com/photos/
    franckmichel/10204691156/in/
    album-72157623794920714

11. Business Meets Pleasure
    Andrew Mager
    flickr.com/photos/
    mager/2561681898/

12. Beyond The Kitsch
    Zemlinki!
    flickr.com/photos/
    zemlinki/498465081/in/
    photostream

13. Real-Life Adventures
    pxhere.com/en/photo/733463

14. Meeting A City
    Fabrizio Sciami
    flickr.com/photos/_
    fabrizio_/15221800008

15. Supermarket Safari
    flickr.com/photos/
    opengridscheduler/16918898859/
    in/photostream

16. We Try Harder
    John Morgan
    flickr.com/photos/
    aidanmorgan/7964542314

17. Smelling Memories
    pexels.com/photo/blur-close-up-
    environment-incense-429918

18. A Better Tourist
    flickr.com/photos/53556792@
    N07/28463649831

19. Perfect Strangers In A Capsule
    Jorge Royan
    commons.wikimedia.org/wiki/File:
    India_-_Kolkata_taxi_-_3771.jpg

20. Festive Rituals
    GoToVan
    flickr.com/photos/
    gotovan/39634768404/in/
    album-72157679742361715

21. Gold In The Mud
    Davidlohr Bueso
    flickr.com/photos/
    daverugby83/4466043347

22. Out On The Edge
    b k
    flickr.com/photos/
    joiseyshowaa/3728426830

23. Go Residential
    rawpixel.com/image/90515

24. There Are Others Here With Us
    Elizaveta Butryn
    commons.wikimedia.org/wiki/
    File:Montmartre,_Sacr%C3%A9-
    Coeur.jpg

25. The Mere Exposure Effect
    ian mcwilliams
    flickr.com/photos/
    supermac/3956838224

26. A Heroic Act Of Willpower
    pxhere.com/en/photo/714580

27. Mental Souvenirs
    Marco Zanferrari
    flickr.com/photos/
    tuttotutto/350018608

28. Back To Reality
    rawpixel.com/image/326873

City view with big wheel
pxhere.com/en/photo/548376

Travellers planning
rawpixel.com/image/57227

Taxi
LawHoiKi
flickr.com/photos/
lawhoiki/15704124991

Residential neighborhood
pxhere.com/en/photo/1410720

Supermarket
pexels.com/photo/assorted-bottle-
and-cans-811108

ABOUT THE AUTHOR

Johan Idema (1973) is a passionate promoter of innovation in the art world. He works as a consultant, writer, and cultural entrepreneur. He specializes in creative concept development, business planning and innovation management – and he likes innovative vacations too.

Johan Idema has worked at several cultural institutions and has extensive experience as an art consultant. He is also a regular public speaker. His recent publications include *Present! – Rethinking Live Classical Music* (2011), which focuses on how to make live classical music more exciting and accessible, and *How to Visit an Art Museum* (2013), which offers a fresh look at how to get the most out of a trip inside a museum.

For more information, please go to: www.johanidema.net

INDEX

INDEX